This book was compiled as an offering for the Vyasa Puja celebration of my spiritual master, 2014.

For comments or inquiries, any reader is hereby warmly invited to correspond with the author:

tilakapublishing@gmail.com

All rights reserved Tilaka Publishing, 2014.

Writing in Relation
To Krishna Consciousness,
Volume 3:

Rediscovering Vrindavan

tad-vag-visargo janantagha-viplav
yasmin prati-slokam abaddhavaty api
namany anantasya yaso 'nkitani yat
srnvanti gayanti grnanti sadhavah

On the other hand, that literature which is full of descriptions of the transcendental glories of the name, fame, forms, past times, etc., of he unlimited Supreme Lord is a different creation, full of transcendental words directed toward bringing about a revolution in the impious lives of this world's misdirected civilization. Such transcendental literatures, even though imperfectly composed, are heard, sung and accepted by purified men who are thoroughly honest.

(Srimad Bhagavatam, 1.5.11)

Introduction, page 6.

Author's note, page 10.

Poems, page 12.

Improvisations, page 59.

A five day diary approaching Janmastami and Srila Prabhupad's appearance day, page 72.

Playing with words, page 80.

Afterword page 85.

Introduction

How this publication came into being this year, I must honestly admit to be solely and wholly by the mercy of guru and Gauranga. At the approach of Vyasa Puja preparations in the month of December, it seemed to me that there would be no book to present to my spiritual master this year. However, as I started to look through this years collection of notebooks and scrambled pieces of paper, a small treasure was unveiled. I took it as Krishna's kind mercy upon His poor, struggling bhakta, to somehow help him along the path of surrendering body, mind and words to the service of Yuga Dharma Harinama Sankirtan, the heart and soul of the modern day guru parampara.

As I go back through vehicle of scattered notes, devotional observations and expressions, to relive this year in devotional service, a theme arises, dawning on the horizon of the heart and mind; a theme of perseverance in the face of obstacles, and how the mercy of the Pancha Tattva makes it appearance even in the lives of the most insignificant creatures in creation. This publication is a statement to this very fact. Even though being a compilation sure to be speckled with faults and misconceptions, the attempt to approach a bona fied spiritual master, through the medium of sadhu sanga, vaishnava seva and harinam sankritan, is to be considered worth while, regardless of failure or success. This is the statement of ISKCON founder acharya Srila A. C. Bhaktivedanta Swami Prabhupada, during his first year alone, as a preacher on the Lower East Side in New York, in 1966:

> *"We are not always successful in our attempts in preaching work but such failures are certainly not ludicrous. In the Absolute field both success and failures are glorious."*
> (Letter to Mangalaniloy brahmachari, 16th July)

Similarly, my own feeble endeavor, although in a category of lightyears, if not eons away from the transcendental character of Srila Prabhupada, which cannot be imitated, is to follow in the lotus footsteps of the same mood of surrender. At least, this is the humble conviction of the insignificant author, who's only honest desire is to share with the reader some of his experiences in an on going life of attempted surrender to the process of devotional service.

Om tat sat.

Author's note

*Be conscious,
I beg,
be conscious,
for anything else
is a waste!*

Poems

After three months of writer's block (5.8.2013).

> *"If he is in constant contact with the Supreme Lord by devotional service, the conditioned living entity also becomes freed from the infections of maya."*
>   (Srimad Bhagavatam 3.28.43, purport)

There is
an infectious substance
in my heart,
a contagion,
somehow incurred
from my
rummaging
around down here
in the
material world.

I am
infected,
diseased.
I'm
not well.

The cure
is service.
How so?
The goswamis

of Vrindavan
serve Krishna
out of
spontaneous attraction.
This is not
my level.
I still struggle
with the
mind an senses.
I am still
heavily identified
with the
false self,
mind and body,
as personality.

Am I
lost, then?

According to
Srila Prabhupada's purport
there is great hope
for redemption,
to free myself
from the ropes of maya,
to regain my inherent
healthy condition.

*"Constant contact
by devotional
service"*
is the cure.

What is that
service,
then?

Early rise,
sixteen rounds in
attempted attentiveness.
Regulated life,
favorable
Vaishnava association
and
kirtan.
The more,
the better.
And,
with whatever
energy and inspiration
that is left
from
devotional family life,
take it to
the streets.
Chant and dance
as a
public display,
confident about
the causeless mercy
of Gaura Nitai
on the
neck bent,
Kali yuga burdened heads
of the
embodied

conditioned souls.

Krishna is
the goal.
Gauranga gives
the process.
Guru gives
the service.

Simply act
and embrace.

A grandmother departs, 09.12.2013.

Dear Grandma,
please accept my most
humble obeisances.
All glories
to Srila Prabhupad.

Although you may not
realize,
this is how devotees of
Krishna
greet each other,
trying to take the
humble position,
for they know of the
exalted position of
activities performed in
devotional service and
they respect the jiva soul.

A century ago,
in the early nineteen hundreds,
when you were young,
the Hare Krishna
movement
had not yet manifested it's
presence in the west,
and even as an
elderly lady,
almost a hundred years later,
as your grandson

took up the path of
Krishna consciousness, you may not
have had so much
understanding of how
this would in any way
affect your life.

Therefore,
I would like to share
with you
some of my tiny
realizations,
hoping to
somehow inform you
of some great mercy
which has
unnoticeably
come your way.

There was a great saint
in India, and after inheriting
his father's kingdom,
at a very young age,
he said that the
family of pure devotees
are greatly benefitted
for many generations,
both passed and
in the future.

Of course,
my devotional practice
is compromised

by a materially conditioned
mentality,
still I have faith
in the words of
king Prahlad.

Dear Grandma,
you may never have
chanted
Hare Krishna,
but know that today
I offered flower garlands
on your behalf to
Gaura Nitai,
Krishna Balaram
and Radhe Shyama
in Vrindavan,
asking Them
to please bless you
with spiritual advancement
toward the
lotus abode of
Radha and Krishna,
the true home
of all souls.

Safe journey,
wherever you may
go.

Christmas preaching spirit, 2013.

Alarm clock
calls me from
a distance,
it's 4:30 am.
Rise,
then bathroom
routine.
Chanting,
struggling with
inattentiveness,
yet following
in the footsteps
of previous acharyas
and contemporary
senior devotees,
attempting to
draw the mind
back to the Names
when it wanders.
This process
is the actual
mercy
of the Krishna consciousness
movement.

In this way,
twelve rounds.

Time has come
for investing in

health:
> *"Keep your health
> in good condition
> and work very hard
> for Krishna."*

Soaked chia seeds,
cow urine on an empty stomach,
spirulina and a spoonful of oil.

Somewhat
invigorated,
preparations for
puja is made.

It's Christmas morning.
I take the warmth
from the sliver lamp
offered to Their Lordships
and hold it to
my head for respect,
then to my heart
out of love.
Washing and drying
paraphernalia.

A piece of maha,
then fifteen minutes
for breakfast,
sandwich with cheese.

Car ride to work.
The mood of the world

is quiet.
Patients of the ward,
being in an unfortunate state,
are in no condition
to jump and dance.
I become occupied
in routine activity.
Eight hours pass,
striving to outwardly
being a gentleman
for the sake of
the good impression.

Returning home
my wife is cooking
a feast.
All is nearly done.
Soothing bath,
tilak on twelve places,
gayatri.
Frying koftas
and making a
traditional norwegian sauce
with juniper berries
to go with them.

There is a preaching
function in our house
on this day.
My dear wife,
always the devotee,
has arranged for
an open evening

for those interested in
experiencing an
alternative festivity.
News of it
even reaches
one of the country's
largest papers.

Kirtan,
then serving feast.
Lord Caitanya showers
His mercy on
all present.
Smiles and friendly
interactions.

Guests leave
10 pm.
Chanting two rounds
I fall asleep,
waking around
1 am to shift
from floor
to sofa.

8 am,
rise.
Again bathroom routine.
Chanting two rounds
from day before,
then writing
this poem.

Let it snow, let it snow, let it snow (January 28th, 2014).

Today is
second day
of clearing the driveway
of our new centre
in Oslo
for snow.
Snowing for ten days straight,
this is that northern
conditioning,
impeccably predictable,
received by many
with ambiguous enthusiasm.

The snowplow
is by all means a
welcome help
in keeping the streets
clear of
this beautiful, yet
encumbering
white mass,
soft and pure, yet
frigid like the clasp of
death.

However,
it seems that
the entrance to our
driveway

is not part of the snowplows'
grand plan
of being the ever
helping hand.
Today
again
it was
blocked,
waist high
and packed,
quite in contrast to the
fluffy, friendly lair
along the path
leading to our door.

I started digging.

The snowplow is much like the mind.
He has a plan,
a fool proof idea
of how to make it
alright and neat,
no problem,
plowing through material enjoyment
like a breeze.
Some obstacle?
No problem,
full throttle and a broad grin
clears all doubts away,
collecting in heaps,
only to leave them aside to continue
on another mission,
waving at passing kids

eyes wide with
expectancy,
gives went to feelings of
great importance
and surely a pillar like,
if not irreplaceable role,
in the upkeep of this
winter age society.

I must keep digging.

I realize
that digging in the
masses,
clearing driveways,
so as to keep the path
home
available,
is a rare blessing
in this neck deep
white muck
of winter landscapes,
of maya.

The snowplow of the mind,
duty bound and persistent,
cannot be easily checked.

I must keep digging.

As long as the
padded boots and
woolen gloves of

previous acharyas' instructions
are worn,
there is indeed protection from the
cold of this age.
Even hours spent
shoveling packed blocks
in the driveway entrance,
my fragile bones
remain warm.

I must keep digging.

The heaps of material desires
seems insurmountable,
yet they melt away,
leaving only bare,
fertile ground behind,
at the coming of
spring.

> *"Of seasons I am flower bearing spring."*

Keep digging,
keep clearing,
keep chanting.

Soul's spring
will come.

Seated amongst the reeds of coastline Denmark, mid september, 2013.

A last sip
of freedom,
in the eyes
of a friend.

Feint whisper
of past pledges,
by coastline view
is seated
windowed you.

Trembling reeds
bent as bows,
who's invisible arrows
make war on
the surging forces
of the almighty wind.

Resolve remains firm.
(*"Not on all levels"*,
whispers someone,
an observing spectator.)

Still,
resolve based on hope,
hope based on faith,
faith based
on taste.
Seemingly endless rows

of reeds,
flailing their bodies
against the surging forces
of almighty wind.

I have no such
courage.
Risking life and
limb is
not my level.

However,
I can serve
as a mere tool
at the practical end
of the specter
of life.

To loose hope
gives no
meaning,
in our philosophy.

Let the mind have
past and future
for selfish
indulgence.

In the now,
there is always
activity.

Mind on paper in park, late autumn, 2013.

Sunset
in the park,
but a spark
of the
beauty
of Krishna.

Golden light
filtering
through
a tree's
thinning leaves.

People pass.
A coated lady with a purse
carries
assorted goods
from the local
supermarket.

A dog
chases a ball.

> *"Nothing new
> under the
> sun",*

they say.

But there
is more.

Tree, lady and
dog,
all vehicles of
a soul.

Although my eyes
perceive
only gross forms,
with the sight
of scripture,
sastra caksus,
true reality
can be ascertained.

Our dear
Srila Prabhupada
has given
his purports
for the next
then thousand years.

Read,
like your life
depends on it.

This is the truth spoken.

Rediscovering Vrindavan, October 2012.

Today I take the time
to just wander around
in Vrindavan.
I search out roads
which I have yet
to venture.
Discovering
a dusty path leading
into the fields
my excitement grows.
Vrindavan adventure.

As I progress on the path
the external sounds
of the Dham
fades into the background.
Peacoks play in the trees:
    "Shyam, Shyam, Shyam."
A few motorbikes,
but besides this
I am alone.

A passing local greets me
with a smile missing a tooth.
A dog slumbers in
the soft Braj raj.

I am half expecting
to find footprints
with auspicious marks
in the dust,

but they are nowhere
to be seen.
Open fields,
scattered trees.
Flocks of birds
soar in the sky
in playful patterns.
Weather is cool
and accommodating
for my Norwegian conditioning.

I am sitting on a rock
observing the scene
for a while:
> *An abandoned tractor*
> *awaits engagement.*
> *A sadhu's home*
> *amidst blossoming*
> *rose bushes.*

Taking it in
wanting to engage my senses
in honoring
this transcendental atmosphere,
I taste a particle of peace.

Again the covering calls me
from a distance:
> *"Bang",*
fireworks, somewhat prematurely,
celebrates the death of Ravana.
A truck puffs forward
on the road behind the trees.

I rise, but
before returning back
I will venture
a little further,
this place is so sweet.

The farmer is back on
his tractor.
I will also
continue my journey,
this life
in the service of
guru and Gauranga.

Into the fields (rediscovering Vrindavan, part 2).

I gaze at
the world,
sitting cross legged,
taking in the scene,
Vrindavan nature.

Dry, crust earth.
Flocks of peacocks
nipping seeds out
of the soil.
A raging farmer
throws rocks and
yells curses, chasing
the birds away,
only to have them
return after he has gone.

I gaze at
the world,
sitting cross legged,
taking in the scene,
hand in beadbag,
Vrindavan nature.

A gathering of peacocks
prance around
in the dry, crisp grass.
Two males
are competing for
the favor of the

fairer sex,
displaying their
feathery pride.
The females seem
oblivious to their
efforts, casually
minding their business,
tending to the chicks.

I gaze at
the world,
sitting cross legged,
taking in the scene,
the afternoon sun
soothing incoming
winter's chill.

A stray dog wants
to usurp my place
of resting, baring
teeth and uttering
growls of attitude.
I show him the stick
and he is taken aback,
but not yet convinced.
I mentally project
beating him on the head
chasing him
away. He gets the point.

I gaze at
the world,
sitting cross legged,

taking in the scene,
a puffing tractor passes,
a kid on a bicycle
calls "Hare Krishna".

For a moment
I reside in
Vrindavan, but
the world calls
and my journey
for today is at its
end.

Remembering Srila Prabhupada, part 1 Juhu beach.

Waves come rolling in,
endlessly
gurgling, almost
like a liquid growl,
friendly yet very powerful.

At this place
Srila Prabhupad would take
his famous morning walks.
Scientists, mayavadis
or any materially engrossed person
would be smashed
to pieces
by the ever merciful acharya.

Years later I am here
at this place of pilgrimage.
Sand is so smooth.
Tide is low.
I adventure to the
brim of the sea
searching for small conch shells.

The ocean is the world
largest body.
It harbors immense power.
Rising,
gathering it's watery masses
from the depths,
by one stroke

it can annihilate civilization.

However,
Srila Prabhupad said it would not.
The ocean will not cross
the boundaries of the shoreline
being arranged and dutifully
complying
with the laws laid down by Krishna.

I am safe on the beach,
for now.
Still, my mind
is there with me.
To not fall victim
to it's whims
I engage it in
Prabhupad smaranam,
as I have seen my Guru Maharaja
on countless occasions
relate past times of Srila Prabhupad,
always relishing
an important point,
or absorbing deeply in remembrance.

For now
I will take my japa walk
in the sands of Juhu beach,
following in the
lotus footsteps
of Srila Prabhupad.

Remembering Srila Prabhupad, part 2 personal quarters at Juhu temple.

"Bombay is my office."

From here
Srila Prabhupad would
conduct his transcendental business,
reaching out in all directions
through the limbs of his
dedicated followers,
to reclaim one and all,
on behalf of his spiritual master,
back to the supreme shelter
of our lost relationship with
Radha and Krishna.

No lacs or crores of rupees,
dollars, pounds or yen
could sufficiently supply
the dire need of this mission.

Still,
Srila Prabhupad would not
force any living entity.

Once,
here in these office rooms
the father of Giriraj Maharaja
visited, having come to
fetch his son home.

The father was a very rich man.
He handed Srila Prabhupad
a blank check,
already signed.
If his son would return with him
back to the States,
Srila Prabhupad could
fill in any numbers
of his choosing.
"Call Giriraj",
Srila Prabhupad said.
Entering the room, Giriraj offered
obeisances.
Srila Prabhupad frankly told him
that his father had come
to invite him home,
to which end he had
presented the blank check.

"What do you want?",
Srila Prabhupad asked the
young brahmachari.
Giriraj said
he was happy serving Prabhupad.

Srila Prabhupad
gave back the check.

My dear Srila Prabhupad,
by some amazing good fortune
I find myself in that same office
on this day.
Was it not for your

expertise in spiritual affairs,
who knows where I would be?

I will stay
with you.

Speaking to the mind, 22.12.2012

It's ok to be
crazy,
just don't turn to
madness or
insanity.

Bring forth radical
ideas, that's fine.
Choose your own
path, that's appropriate.

But,
don't concoct meaning
or speculate your own
purports.
Don't ignore Vaishnava
sanga, or
presume to assume an
important position
or
influential post.

We are not the doers.
We are not this
body or mind.

Follow Srila Prabhupada
faithfully.
Serve the Vaishnavas.

Please remember,
chant Hare Krishna
with attention.

Speaking to the mind 2, date unknown.

There is
certainly
many
great devotees
in this
Krishna consciousness
movement.

For my part
I am trying
to serve them
in some,
or any
capacity.

Mind:
> *"My dear Krishna,*
> *my path*
> *is strewn*
> *with thorns.*
> *I bleed*
> *and it's a pain.*
> *Release me."*

This may be
and has been
said
in my existence.

Know these

facts,
however:
Thorns strewn
are spread
by hand
> *(thorns don't manifest*
> *by themselves).*

Carefully
harvested,
one by one,
from the
weeds and creepers
of the heart of
self proclaimed
centre.

Believe
in disbelief,
but do not
yield.

Hold
the
line!
Remain.

Mind
is always
there, yes.

Chant
and maintain
a happy mood.

Beam me up Krishna, 26.09.2012.

Death is like
a portal.
It opens for
opportunities
to transfer
to any desired
destination.

This said,
to travel through
this medium
is not a cheap thing.

Without the correct
identification,
transportation
is forced upon the
living being
by the accumulated
karmic debt
one has acquired,
and the designated end
of such a journey
is most uncertain.

To truly unlock
the secret of this
portal,
one must engage
wholeheartedly

in Krishna consciousness,
for only by the grace
of the Lord
and His magnanimous devotees,
can the intense greed
for devotional service,
the only valid ticket
for Goloka Vrindavan,
be purchased,
so that the passage
will be a safe one.

I beg to commence
this journey.
I long for this
currency.

Awaiting my qualification,
I will remain loyal
and active
in reminding
any fellow traveler
about the supreme reality
of this destination.

Heartache and honesty (Radhastami, 12:05am, 2013).

Part 1:

Rarely do i
realize
what a fool
I am.

Rarely do i
recognize
how cruel
I am.

Rarely do I
emphasize
qualities
of others.

To often
I am
worshiping
myself as
the centre.

Rarely do I,
if ever,
glorify
my friend the Name
with any true
feeling or
heart.

Part 2:

Thus is my demonic state. This is my testimony. Of all ungrateful creatures of this world, I have certainly earned my rank and position by freedom of choice. Even now, there is no real safety from my indulgence in the lower modes. In mind I nurture desires and make plans for abominations. Even though a disgrace, I am allowed to continue. How is this so? I torture myself, crushing any tiny glimpse of goodness under the sharp heel of so called self pity. Is it truth, or have I deceived myself all this time?

In all honesty, I cannot find my way. I am lost to myself. I see all as dark. Still I am allowed to continue. Why is this so? Willfully, I break my vows with plans for concealment, for running and hiding. Willfully, I take to harsh words in confusion. I cannot help myself. Expression of the rightful heart is so much covered, I cannot see it for the best of me. How is it that I am allowed to continue? I strike down any voice which raises questions towards my pardon with the oiled sword of uncertainty. Is this truth, or have I deceived myself all this time?

Part 3:

The body
ends
with death.
For the soul
this is merely
a change
of dress.

The mind
is the inner
garment,
closest to the
touch.

The disease
of identification's
roots
have found
nourishment
in the core
of my heart.

Only Krishna's
Name
can save me now.

To be beyond
redemption
is just another
trick
of puffed up

false ego.
However,
to grasp
such an
opportunity,
is a test of
courage
and
deed.

Many a battle
is already lost.
Treasury
ransacked.
Supplies
poisoned.
Gates barred
from the outside.

Trapped in a carnal fortress
escape
is made possible
only from
within.

The Name.

The Name!

Soon come
the dazzling
sunrise
of soul's

hope.
This is
guaranteed
by proof of
practice
and scripture.

Prepare
for embrace,
love is as real
as reality
itself.

Dare to feel,
to love,
for none
can ever
force your
hand
in motion.

Dare to trust,
to search,
for your
destination
is in tune
with your
heart of hearts,
believe it.

Dear guru maharaja,
please forgive me,
but I truly wish

to render some
service.

Brokenhearted
and utterly
shameful
I bow
and clasp your
lotus feet
in desperation.

Will I
remain?

The Name.

Krishna!

Improvisations

Improvisations, an introduction

Improvisations recorded here are of two categories. One is written in the flow of a moments inspiration. The other is more constructed, in the sense that it is more dwelled upon, yet still minimized and tuned in to an idea or a moment, as described in the former category. Editing is purposely kept to a minimum, and the format itself is given for emphasizing key words, aiming at increased and more condensed expression. At least, this is the hope of the insignificant author.

For me, improvisations are attempts at naked honesty in the spur of a seconds fleeting impression or experience, be it a feeling or perhaps a meeting by chance, and somehow reaching out, with trembling hands, and in mind's humility trying to somehow reel it in, for Krishna conscious reflection.

Above all, improvisations are written experiments of the heart and devotional mind. They are attempts at service, words molded from bare unedited substance of a desire to somehow serve the spiritual master by pleasing the Vaishnavas, and creating a platform from which bhakti yoga, devotional service to Krishna, can take on a poetic form, available to anyone.

If nothing else is achieved, there is at least the time spent contemplating the instructions of guru, sastra and sadhu, begging for mercy.

Improvisations I

Remember
the accumulative
darkness.

Remember
that night time
of the heart.

Shun
it's presence.
Avoid
it's association.

If nothing else
seek mental
shelter
at the lotus feet
of guru.

Seek out
some humble
service.
Take
early rest
to rise
for good rounds.

Embrace.
Impress
upon the mind
this instruction.

Improvisations II

Sadhu sanga
makes
all the
difference.

Serve
the saints.

Go
overboard,
make it
special.

It
is
special.

Time
is
crucial.

There
is great
need
and urgency.

Time wasted
is a
massacre
of

good will
given.

Refuse.
Resist.
Remain
loyal.

Count
blessings
received.

Remind
the mind
to mind
it's
surroundings.

The blessing
is
the process.

Endeavor
matters.

Guru
matches
the heart.
Believe.

Improvisations III

3:15 am
alarm clock.

Press
snooze.

4:45 am.
Emerging
from under
my quilt.

Forest sanga
with prabhus
during weekend.

Come Monday;
inspired,
but
tired.

Felt bad
about
meager six rounds
before departure
for work.

Slept
on the
train.
Plus two

rounds
only.

On my
heels
during day,
but
forest association
and sixteen degree
lake snan
from weekend
maintained
my spirit.

Work day
ends.
Overcast sky
with rain
observed
from train.

Again
facing Krishna
in japa,
I am
caught
off guard.

Chanting
is enlivening.
Fatigued
mind
transcended.

Sweetness
of the
Names
manifest.

Thankful
for Krishna's
kind
reciprocation,
I write
this
poem
going home.

Improvisations IV

There is
duty
and then there is
love.

Duty is
unavoidable
by
definition.

Love is
a
choice.

Duty
you perform
with
detachment
to result.
Duty is
regulated,
defined
by category.
Duty is
technical application
of
laws and
injunctions.

Love

however,
is
unbound
and
beyond.

Love is
unbreakable attachment
to
and feelings
of
the heart.

Experiencing
neglect
or
rejection,
is the
peak
of ecstasy.

No rules.
No limits.
No time,
or
space,
in love.

Only surrender.
Choose
surrender.

Improvisation V

Mind.
Unwelcome
attraction.
Laziness.

This
prescription
breeds
trouble.

Tested
and
approved.

Certified.

Shelter
is needed.
Shelter
is given,
so gratitude
is needed.
Gratitude
spawns from
humility.
Humility
is birthed
by purity.
Purity
is received

in association
with vaishnavas.

Seek out
the vaishnavas.

How to
associate?

Through
service.

A five day diary approaching Janmastami and Srila Prabhupada's appearance day

Day 1, Sunday 25th August, 2013
(11:20 pm)

Went for an hour run. Aindra prabhu blasting Maha Mantra the whole way. Why do I run? It is not for an athletic body. It is for health. What health? Its is a myth, Srila Prabhupada would sometimes say. This may be true. Still, I need endurance and energy for preaching and dancing in the kirtan. For lasting in kirtan. And by the mercy of the Vaishnavas, if I can hold body and mind together with soul in a beneficial way, there may become an opportunity for dedication at the end of life. Sannyas? What good is traveling and preaching, if the body is already gone? So these are my reflections around my one hour run this evening. Tomorrow is another day. Another run. Early rise and chant.

Day 2, Monday 26th August, 2013
(11:32 pm)

Today also an hour run. Coming back from work in the afternoon, my wife has cooked dinner; kinoa and sautéed vegetables. Being tired after a long day I fall asleep on the couch for two hours. Waking up, my mind made some resistance, but I persevered. Ran and felt good after. Much like poison in the beginning and nectar in the end. If only I could bring the same mentality to devotional service. I am such a lazy fellow, and my mind keeps seducing me, like a witch's lullaby, hypnotic slumber. A trap! My great deliverance is harinam sankirtan. We go out regularly now. Goal is every day, one hour after work, but in reality it is more like four to five times a week. Still pretty good. All I want is that guru maharaja will be pleased. Continue and remain loyal.

Day 3, Tuesday 27th August, 2013
(11:50 pm)

"Whatever is rightly done, however humble, is noble"
- Sir Henry Royce

Today is one of those days where the conditioned nature of my false ego and it's endless attachments become disturbingly visible and factual. The mind, drenched in the lower modes of nature, revolts and causes such an embarrassing scene. I become upset, frustrated, and maybe most of all disappointed about my endurance and spiritual perseverance. So much for running! Reduced to a crawling beast, cowering in the shadows, I am plunged deeply into the frigid pool of despair. My only solace is prayer: "Krishna, if you are out there, please help me."

Literally minutes later, I am contacted by a devotee stranded at Oslo airport in transit to Helsinki. And so on a silver plate Vaishnava seva and sanga is served, and all seeming difficulties disappear. It all ends with me going to the airport just before midnight, bringing a nice Vaishnava back to our home to stay for a few days, arranging prasadam and bed linen, and boiling water for tea. With a wave of His magic wand, Krishna showers His causeless mercy on this wretched beast, finding him engagement. Suddenly, surrender is easy.

Day 4, Wednesday 28th August (Sri Krishna Janmastami), 2013
(11:25 pm)

Another late evening. Celebration continues in the local temple. Unfortunately, I am tired and have got an early start tomorrow. Lately, I have been carrying many a worry in my mind. Meditating on them, feeds their repeated appearance. A devotee once asked Srila Prabhupad: *"What is the difference between the mind and the intelligence?"* Srila Prabhupad replied: *"Standing on a balcony the mind says JUMP, but the intelligence says DON'T."*

Dear Srila Prabhupad,
I am trying to do something for your mission, but I find myself too caught up in the mind. Conclusion is to engage in mantra; early rise with good rounds, and harinam sankirtan. Please if you desire it, help me stay focused on the goal, serving Krishna and His devotees, and never loose sight.

Day 5, Thursday 29th August (Srila Prabhupad's appearance day), 2013
(00:40 am)

My dear Srila Prabhupad,

Please accept my humble obeisances. All glories to guru and Gauranga.

There are so many things that can be said about your amazing gift to the world at large. Harinam sankirtan is here to stay as a global phenomenon. All thanks to your efforts, single handedly taking the mission of Lord Caitanya, on the order of Srila Bhaktisiddhanta Maharaja, and broadcasting it far and wide. Your empowered followers are continuing this legacy even today, as Hare Krishna has become a household word, a cultural entity or a reputed faith.

You are a great hero. You are so much more, more than I can possibly fathom or imagine. Still, for my level, you are there as Srila Prabhupad, that deep and gentle soul, always aware and alert, always profound and wise. A scholar, a saint, a simple person with a great vision including everyone.

Thank you for including me.

Always the aspiring servant of your servant's servant,

Yudhisthira das

Playing with words

Playing with words 1, Vrindavan 2012.

Advancement:

> *Years spent*
> *being patient,*
> *however,*
> *not applied to the same extent*
> *in the age of Kali, hellbent,*
> *really only dependent*
> *on the All Merciful*
> *Effulgent,*
> *coming in His golden advent.*

Playing with words 2, Vrindavan 2012

Authorized:

> *Legalized*
> *action wise,*
> *synthesized*
> *so as to*
> *conceptualize*
> *our daily life.*

Playing with words 3, Vrindavan 2012

Attachment:

> *Solely meant*
> *for the Lord*
> *three places bent,*
> *in all honesty*
> *is only sent*
> *by divine decent.*

Afterword

By nature I observe the world around me. I scry for meaning, for something that will stand out and tell me that this is worth while. In my desperate state, I hunger for that evasive feeling of satisfaction, of quenching ones thirst, knowing for certain that my current investment will have a lasting effect, not just sand straining between trembling fingers, realizing that I have only just wasted my time for nothing. No one wants this. We all seek nourishment and emotional fulfillment. *Ananda mayo bhyasat.*

This publication has been dedicated to that search. The treasure hunt of the heart, which we in honest reality are all pursuing. I have wasted so much time, time which is forever spent and which is never to be replenished. Fortunately, by my contact with the Vaishnavas, especially my dear spiritual master, living entities loyal in their service to Sri Krishna, I have been blessed with inspiration for coming closer to that reality myself. How I qualified for this gift cannot be estimated, because it does not exist. There is only causeless mercy, and nothing else.

In gratitude, I have commenced this quest. In gratefulness, I preserver. In utter helplessness, I hope, beyond hope, to somehow please these magnanimous personalities, roaming this swirling globe called Earth, only for the benefit of the fallen peoples in this ongoing age of Kali, an age where hypocrisy and deceit are acclaimed virtues, and a spiritual approach toward life is seen as highly objectionable, if not madness.

Any kind reader is hereby offered a benediction, by the insignificant author. May you find out Krishna in your life, and be ever engaged in loving interactions with His devotees. I too long for this, and by endeavoring to lease this fortune, this real life treasure, to one and all, there is every chance, by the grace of guru and Gauranga, that the same opportunity may be presented to me.

Hare Krishna

Herstellung und Verlag:
BoD - Books on Demand, Norderstedt
ISBN 978-3-7357-1905-8